Table of Contents

.... 1

Chapter 1: Understanding Your Financial Situation 3

1.1 Assessing Your Current Financial Status 4

1.2 Identifying Sources of Income and Expenses 6

1.3 Analyzing Your Debt and Liabilities 9

1.4 Setting Clear Financial Goals 12

Chapter 2: Creating a Budget for Success 15

2.1 The Importance of Budgeting 16

2.2 Developing a Realistic Budget 18

2.3 Allocating Funds for Saving and Investing 21

2.4 Strategies for Sticking to Your Budget 24

Chapter 3: Building an Emergency Fund and Managing Debt 27

3.1 Establishing an Emergency Fund 28

3.2 Understanding Different Types of Debt 30

3.3 Developing a Debt Repayment Plan 33

3.4 Tips for Avoiding Debt Traps 36

Chapter 4: Mastering the Art of Saving and Investing 39

4.1 Understanding the Power of Saving 40

4.2 Exploring Different Investment Options 43

4.3 Creating a Diversified Investment Portfolio 46
4.4 Managing Risks and Market Volatility 49
Chapter 5: Navigating Major Financial Decisions 52
5.1 Buying vs. Renting: Making the Right Choice 53
5.2 Understanding Mortgages and Homeownership 56
5.3 Planning for Retirement and Long-Term Savings 60
5.4 Making Informed Insurance Choices 63
Chapter 6: Achieving Long-Term Financial Freedom 66
6.1 Setting Long-Term Financial Goals 67
6.2 Strategies for Increasing Income 70
6.3 Reviewing and Adjusting Your Financial Plan 73
6.4 Embracing a Debt-Free Lifestyle 77
Conclusion: Sustaining Your Financial Freedom Journey 81

Financial Freedom

Achieving Your Goals and Living Debt Free

Copyright ©

Chapter 1: Understanding Your Financial Situation

1.1 Assessing Your Current Financial Status

In the journey towards achieving financial freedom, the first crucial step is to assess your current financial status. It's like laying the foundation of a sturdy house – without a clear understanding of where you stand financially, you'll have a hard time building a strong future. This process may seem daunting at first, but with dedication and attention to detail, you can gain valuable insights that will help shape your path towards a debt-free and prosperous life.

To begin the assessment, gather all your financial documents, from bank statements to credit card bills and investment account summaries. Create a comprehensive inventory of your assets and liabilities. Your assets may include cash, savings accounts, investments, real estate, and any valuable possessions, while your liabilities encompass debts like credit card balances, student loans, mortgages, and personal loans. It's essential to have a clear picture of both to understand your net worth accurately.

Once you have your financial documents at hand, organize them in a systematic manner, preferably using spreadsheets or financial management tools. Create separate categories for income and expenses, detailing each source of income and itemizing all your expenses, no matter how minor they might seem. Having a comprehensive breakdown of your financial inflows and outflows will help you identify spending patterns and areas where you can potentially cut back.

Next, evaluate your cash flow and understand the balance between your income and expenses. Are you spending more than you earn, or do you have some surplus left at the end of each month? Analyzing your cash flow will give you a clear indication of your financial health and the potential to save or invest more to achieve your goals.

As you delve deeper into your financial assessment, pay close attention to your debt profile. Identify the types of debts you carry, such as high-interest credit cards, student loans, or a mortgage. Analyze the outstanding balances, interest rates, and minimum monthly payments for each debt. Understanding the nature of your debts will help you develop a debt repayment strategy later on.

Furthermore, take note of your credit score. Your credit score is a crucial aspect of your financial life and can impact your ability to secure loans or favorable interest rates. You can obtain your credit score from credit reporting agencies and review your credit report for any errors or discrepancies that might affect your score negatively.

Besides assessing your financial numbers, consider your financial goals and aspirations. Reflect on what you hope to achieve in the short term and long term – be it buying a house, starting a business, or retiring early. Understanding your goals will shape your financial planning and guide you towards making informed decisions.

Be honest with yourself during this assessment process. It's natural to feel uneasy when facing financial realities, especially if you're in debt or have not saved as much as you intended. However, remember that acknowledging your current situation is the first step towards improvement. Stay committed and motivated, knowing that you have the power to change your financial future.

Finally, seek advice and guidance from financial experts if needed. Consulting with a financial advisor can provide valuable insights and personalized strategies tailored to your unique circumstances. They can help you make informed decisions and optimize your financial plan for success.

1.2 Identifying Sources of Income and Expenses

As you progress on your journey to achieve financial freedom and live a debt-free life, a critical step is to identify your sources of income and expenses. Understanding the inflow and outflow of your money is fundamental to effective financial management. By gaining a clear picture of your financial streams, you can make informed decisions, optimize your budget, and work towards your financial goals.

Let's start by examining the various sources of income. Your income includes the money you earn from different avenues, such as your primary job, secondary employment, freelance work, or any passive income streams, like dividends, rental properties, or investments. Take the time to list all your income sources and calculate the total monthly or yearly income. This exercise will help you see the bigger picture of your earning potential and give you insight into areas where you can potentially increase your income.

Next, delve into your expenses and categorize them for better understanding. Start by organizing your expenses into essential and non-essential categories. Essential expenses encompass necessities like housing, utilities, groceries, transportation, insurance, and healthcare. Non-essential expenses, on the other hand, include discretionary spending, such as dining out, entertainment, and impulse purchases. Breaking down your expenses in this manner will highlight areas where you can potentially cut back to increase your savings.

When analyzing your expenses, also consider your fixed and variable expenses. Fixed expenses remain consistent each month and are usually contractual, like rent or mortgage payments, subscription services, and loan installments. Variable expenses, on the other hand, fluctuate month to month and may include items like groceries, fuel, and entertainment. Understanding the difference between fixed and variable expenses will enable you to create a budget that accounts for both.

To gain a comprehensive view of your spending patterns, track your expenses diligently for a few months. Keep receipts, review bank statements, and use budgeting apps or spreadsheets to record every expenditure. This practice will help you identify any spending leaks and give you a realistic overview of your financial habits.

Remember that identifying sources of income and expenses is not a one-time task but an ongoing process. As your financial situation evolves, so will your income and expenses. Make it a habit to regularly review and update your budget to reflect any changes in your life circumstances, such as salary increases, job changes, or new financial commitments.

In addition to assessing your current income and expenses, consider ways to diversify your income sources. Explore potential side hustles or investment opportunities that align with your skills and interests. The more diversified your income streams, the more resilient your finances will be in the face of economic uncertainties.

While striving to increase your income, also focus on reducing unnecessary expenses. Evaluate your spending habits and identify areas where you can cut back without sacrificing your quality of life. Small changes in your daily routines, such as preparing meals at home, using public transportation, or negotiating better deals on services, can add up to significant savings over time.

Identifying sources of income and expenses is not just about crunching numbers; it's about gaining a deeper understanding of your financial behavior and making intentional choices to improve your financial health. By knowing where your money comes from and where it goes, you gain the power to shape your financial future. Stay committed to this process, remain open to learning and adjusting, and you'll be on your way to achieving your financial goals and living a debt-free life.

1.3 Analyzing Your Debt and Liabilities

When pursuing financial freedom and aiming to live a debt-free life, it is essential to face your debts and liabilities head-on. Debt is a common financial burden that can impede your progress towards achieving your goals and limit your ability to build wealth. However, by analyzing your debt and liabilities with clarity and determination, you can develop a strategic plan to overcome them and pave the way for a more secure financial future.

Begin the process of debt analysis by creating a comprehensive list of all your debts and liabilities. This includes credit card balances, student loans, personal loans, auto loans, mortgages, and any other outstanding debts. Record the principal amount owed, the interest rate, the minimum monthly payments, and the remaining term for each debt. Having a detailed debt inventory will provide you with a clear overview of your financial obligations and help you prioritize which debts to tackle first.

Once you have your debt list, categorize your debts into high-interest and low-interest debts. High-interest debts typically come with higher interest rates, such as credit card debts, while low-interest debts may include student loans or mortgages. High-interest debts can be more detrimental to your financial well-being, as they accumulate interest at a faster rate, potentially leading to a debt spiral. Therefore, it is often advisable to focus on paying off high-interest debts as quickly as possible.

Next, analyze your cash flow and budget to determine how much you can allocate towards debt repayment each month. Consider your income, expenses, and savings goals to assess how much surplus you can dedicate to debt reduction. While it might be tempting to use all available funds towards debt, remember to strike a balance between debt repayment and building an emergency fund and savings for other financial goals.

With a clear understanding of your cash flow and the amount available for debt repayment, explore various debt repayment strategies. One popular approach is the snowball method, where you prioritize paying off the smallest debts first while making minimum payments on other debts. As you pay off each debt, the amount available for the next debt increases, creating momentum like a snowball rolling downhill. Another strategy is the avalanche method, where you focus on paying off the highest interest debts first, potentially saving more money on interest payments in the long run.

Consider the option of debt consolidation if you have multiple high-interest debts. Debt consolidation involves combining multiple debts into a single loan with a lower interest rate, making it more manageable to repay. However, be cautious about using consolidation as a quick fix, as it may not address the underlying issues causing debt accumulation.

While analyzing your debt, also explore opportunities for negotiating with creditors or lenders. In some cases, you may be able to negotiate for lower interest rates, reduced payments, or a repayment plan that better suits your current financial situation. Remember that creditors often prefer to receive some payment rather than none, so they may be willing to work with you to find a feasible solution.

Beyond analyzing your debts, it is crucial to assess your overall financial health and identify potential risk areas. Review your credit report regularly to ensure its accuracy and detect any fraudulent activities. A strong credit report is essential for obtaining favorable interest rates on loans and accessing various financial products.

Additionally, consider the impact of debt on your overall financial goals and lifestyle. High levels of debt can hinder your ability to save for emergencies, invest for the future, or achieve major life milestones, such as buying a home or starting a family. Analyzing your debt will give you the motivation to make necessary changes and work towards a more prosperous and fulfilling future.

1.4 Setting Clear Financial Goals

Setting clear and well-defined financial goals is a fundamental step in achieving financial freedom and living a debt-free life. Without a roadmap to guide your financial decisions and actions, it's easy to lose focus and fall into the trap of aimless spending and debt accumulation. By establishing specific, measurable, achievable, relevant, and time-bound (SMART) financial goals, you can align your efforts and resources towards creating a secure and prosperous future.

Begin the process of setting financial goals by reflecting on your aspirations and values. What does financial freedom mean to you? Is it the ability to retire early, travel the world, start a business, or provide a comfortable life for your family? Understanding your motivations and desires will help you craft goals that truly resonate with your life's purpose and vision.

Once you have a clear sense of your aspirations, start by setting short-term, medium-term, and long-term financial goals. Short-term goals may include building an emergency fund, paying off a credit card debt, or saving for a vacation. Medium-term goals could involve saving for a down payment on a house, funding a child's education, or starting a business. Long-term goals encompass objectives like achieving financial independence, retiring comfortably, or leaving a lasting legacy.

When formulating your financial goals, make sure they are specific and measurable. Instead of setting a vague goal like "save more money," set a specific target, such as "save $10,000 for a down payment on a house within two years." Being specific allows you to track your progress and adjust your actions accordingly.

Furthermore, ensure that your goals are achievable and realistic. While it's essential to dream big, setting overly ambitious goals that are beyond your current means might lead to frustration and disappointment. Consider your current financial situation, income, and expenses, and set goals that challenge you while still being attainable with effort and dedication.

Relevance is another critical aspect of setting financial goals. Align your goals with your values and priorities to ensure they bring fulfillment and meaning to your life. A goal that is personally meaningful is more likely to motivate you to stay on track, especially during challenging times.

To add a sense of urgency and commitment to your goals, set specific timeframes for achieving them. A goal without a deadline is merely a wish. Time-bound goals create a sense of accountability and encourage you to take consistent action to move closer to your objectives.

As you define your financial goals, break them down into actionable steps. Each goal should have a clear plan outlining the necessary actions and resources required to accomplish it. For instance, if your goal is to pay off a student loan, devise a repayment plan that includes allocating a certain amount each month to tackle the debt systematically.

Regularly review and reassess your financial goals as your circumstances evolve. Life is dynamic, and your priorities may shift over time. Be open to adjusting your goals if necessary, and celebrate your progress along the way. Recognizing and celebrating even small achievements will keep you motivated and focused on your financial journey.

It's also helpful to share your financial goals with a trusted partner, friend, or family member. Having someone to support and hold you accountable can make a significant difference in staying committed to your goals.

Lastly, be prepared for challenges and setbacks. The path to financial freedom may not always be smooth, and you may encounter unexpected hurdles. Embrace these challenges as learning opportunities and keep your eye on the bigger picture. Stay persistent and resilient, knowing that every step you take brings you closer to your dreams.

Chapter 2: Creating a Budget for Success

2.1 The Importance of Budgeting

Budgeting is a fundamental financial tool that plays a central role in achieving financial freedom and living a debt-free life. It serves as a powerful roadmap for managing your money, enabling you to take control of your finances and make informed decisions about how you spend, save, and invest.

At its core, budgeting involves creating a detailed plan for allocating your income towards different expenses, savings, and financial goals. It acts as a financial compass, helping you navigate through life's complexities and uncertainties with confidence and purpose. Regardless of your current financial situation, whether you're just starting to build wealth or working towards debt repayment, budgeting is a vital step towards financial success.

One of the primary reasons budgeting is so crucial is that it provides you with a clear picture of your financial inflows and outflows. By understanding how much money you earn and where it goes, you can identify potential areas of overspending and find opportunities to save. This awareness helps you avoid living paycheck to paycheck and allows you to plan for unexpected expenses, such as emergencies or major life events.

Budgeting also empowers you to set and achieve financial goals effectively. Whether you aim to pay off debts, save for a dream vacation, buy a home, or retire comfortably, a well-crafted budget can help you allocate resources strategically towards these objectives. It provides the discipline needed to stay on track, making your aspirations more attainable.

Additionally, budgeting instills financial discipline and cultivates mindful spending habits. It encourages you to think critically about each purchase, considering its significance and impact on your overall financial well-being. When you have a budget, you are less likely to indulge in impulsive spending, and you become more intentional about directing your money towards things that genuinely matter to you.

For those burdened by debt, budgeting is a powerful tool for debt management and repayment. By allocating a portion of your income to debt reduction each month, you can systematically chip away at outstanding balances, inching closer to a debt-free life. Budgeting also helps prevent the accumulation of more debt, as you become more aware of your financial limitations and strive to live within your means.

Another significant benefit of budgeting is its ability to reduce financial stress and anxiety. Financial worries are a leading cause of stress for many individuals, impacting overall well-being and personal relationships. A well-structured budget can provide a sense of financial security, knowing that you have a plan to address your financial obligations and work towards your goals.

Furthermore, budgeting enables you to track your progress over time. As you consistently follow your budget, you can monitor how your financial situation evolves and make necessary adjustments along the way. This data-driven approach allows you to make informed decisions about your financial future, optimizing your strategy for better results.

Budgeting is not about restricting yourself from enjoying life or depriving yourself of essential needs. Instead, it's about finding balance and aligning your spending with your values and long-term objectives. When done right, budgeting empowers you to live more intentionally, directing your resources towards what brings you true joy and fulfillment.

2.2 Developing a Realistic Budget

Creating a realistic budget is a cornerstone of effective financial management. It is the process of carefully planning and allocating your income to cover your expenses, savings, and financial goals in a balanced and sustainable manner. A well-designed budget serves as a roadmap for your financial journey, guiding you towards financial freedom and debt-free living.

To develop a realistic budget, you must first gather all relevant financial information. Start by examining your income sources, which may include your salary, freelance earnings, rental income, dividends, or any other sources of money coming into your household. It is essential to have a comprehensive understanding of your total monthly or annual income.

Next, meticulously list all your expenses, taking into account both essential and non-essential items. Essential expenses consist of necessities like housing, utilities, groceries, transportation, insurance, and healthcare. Non-essential expenses include discretionary spending on items such as entertainment, dining out, and impulse purchases. Ensure that your expense list is comprehensive and includes even minor expenses, as they can add up over time.

As you categorize your expenses, consider differentiating between fixed and variable expenses. Fixed expenses are recurring costs that remain relatively stable each month, such as rent or mortgage payments and subscription services. Variable expenses fluctuate from month to month and include items like groceries, fuel, and leisure activities. Understanding the difference between fixed and variable expenses will help you identify areas where you can potentially reduce costs when necessary.

While crafting your budget, be realistic about your spending habits and financial limitations. Avoid the temptation to underestimate expenses or overestimate your income. A realistic budget reflects your actual financial situation and ensures that your goals are attainable. It is essential to strike a balance between budgeting conservatively and allowing room for unexpected expenses.

Remember to factor in savings and investments when developing your budget. Allocate a portion of your income towards building an emergency fund, contributing to retirement accounts, and pursuing other financial objectives. Paying yourself first through savings is a critical habit for achieving long-term financial security.

To ensure that your budget remains realistic and effective, regularly review and adjust it as needed. Life circumstances change, and your financial priorities may shift over time. Be flexible and adaptable, updating your budget to reflect any changes in your income, expenses, or financial goals.

An essential aspect of budgeting is monitoring your spending behavior. Track your expenses diligently and use budgeting apps or spreadsheets to record every transaction. Regularly review your spending patterns to identify any areas where you might be overspending or areas where you can potentially cut back.

During the process of developing a realistic budget, communication and collaboration with your family or household members are vital. Involve everyone in the budgeting process and discuss financial goals collectively. When everyone is on the same page, it becomes easier to maintain financial harmony and work towards shared objectives.

Be prepared for occasional setbacks or deviations from your budget. Life is unpredictable, and unforeseen expenses may arise. Instead of viewing these situations as failures, treat them as learning opportunities. Make adjustments as needed and continue to follow your budgeting principles diligently.

Lastly, don't forget to reward yourself for sticking to your budget and achieving financial milestones. Celebrate your progress, no matter how small, and use positive reinforcement to stay motivated on your financial journey.

2.3 Allocating Funds for Saving and Investing

One of the most critical aspects of achieving financial freedom and building long-term wealth is allocating funds for saving and investing. Saving and investing are two distinct yet interconnected components of a well-rounded financial plan. They provide the means to grow your money, secure your future, and work towards a debt-free life.

When it comes to saving, the primary focus is on setting aside a portion of your income for emergencies and short-term goals. An emergency fund acts as a financial safety net, providing you with a buffer against unexpected expenses, such as medical emergencies, car repairs, or sudden job loss. Without an emergency fund, you may be forced to rely on credit cards or loans, derailing your progress towards financial freedom.

Ideally, an emergency fund should cover three to six months' worth of living expenses. This amount may vary based on individual circumstances, such as job stability and family responsibilities. When determining the size of your emergency fund, consider factors like monthly expenses, insurance coverage, and any other potential sources of financial support.

Once you've established an emergency fund, shift your focus towards saving for short-term goals. These goals may include saving for a vacation, purchasing a new car, or renovating your home. Allocate funds each month towards these objectives and set a timeline for achieving them. Having specific short-term savings goals can keep you motivated and disciplined in your saving habits.

In addition to saving, investing plays a pivotal role in growing your wealth over the long term. Investing involves putting your money to work in various financial assets with the expectation of generating a return on your investment. Common investment vehicles include stocks, bonds, mutual funds, exchange-traded funds (ETFs), real estate, and retirement accounts like IRAs and 401(k)s.

When allocating funds for investing, consider your risk tolerance and investment objectives. Different investments carry varying levels of risk, with higher risk typically associated with the potential for higher returns. It's essential to diversify your investment portfolio to spread risk across different asset classes and industries. Diversification helps mitigate the impact of any one investment's poor performance on your overall portfolio.

If you're new to investing, seek guidance from a financial advisor to help you build a suitable investment strategy based on your goals, risk tolerance, and time horizon. A financial advisor can provide valuable insights, recommend investment options, and help you stay disciplined during market fluctuations.

Keep in mind that investing is a long-term endeavor. The stock market and other investment markets may experience fluctuations in the short term, but historically, they have shown a positive trend over time. Avoid making impulsive decisions based on short-term market movements, and instead, focus on staying committed to your long-term investment strategy.

An essential aspect of allocating funds for saving and investing is automating the process. Set up automatic transfers to your savings and investment accounts each time you receive your paycheck. Automating your finances ensures that you consistently contribute towards your financial goals, even if you're tempted to spend the money on non-essential items.

Regularly review and rebalance your investment portfolio to ensure it remains aligned with your financial goals and risk tolerance. As your life circumstances change, you may need to adjust your investment strategy to reflect new objectives or priorities.

2.4 Strategies for Sticking to Your Budget

Creating a budget is an essential first step in managing your finances, but the real challenge lies in sticking to it. Without discipline and commitment, a budget can easily fall by the wayside, leading to overspending, debt accumulation, and a lack of progress towards your financial goals. Fortunately, there are several effective strategies to help you stay on track and maintain control over your finances.

Set Realistic Goals: When developing your budget, ensure that your financial goals are realistic and achievable. Unrealistic goals can lead to frustration and a lack of motivation. Break down your long-term objectives into smaller, manageable milestones, and celebrate your progress along the way. This sense of achievement will keep you motivated to continue working towards your bigger goals.

Track Your Expenses: Regularly track your expenses to ensure that you are staying within your budget. Keep a record of all your spending, whether through budgeting apps, spreadsheets, or a simple pen and paper. Monitoring your expenses will help you identify areas where you might be overspending and make necessary adjustments.

Prioritize Your Spending: Differentiate between needs and wants and prioritize your spending accordingly. Focus on covering essential expenses, such as housing, utilities, groceries, and debt repayment, before allocating funds towards discretionary items. By aligning your spending with your priorities, you ensure that your money goes towards what truly matters to you.

Use Cash or Debit Cards: Consider using cash or debit cards for your daily spending instead of credit cards. Paying with cash or a debit card forces you to stick to your budgeted amount for each category and reduces the temptation to overspend. Additionally, it helps you avoid accruing credit card debt and the accompanying interest charges.

Practice Delayed Gratification: When tempted to make impulsive purchases, practice delayed gratification. Wait for a day or two before making non-essential purchases. Often, this waiting period gives you time to reconsider the necessity of the item and prevents impulse spending.

Build an Emergency Fund: Having an emergency fund can prevent you from derailing your budget when unexpected expenses arise. Aim to build an emergency fund equivalent to three to six months' worth of living expenses. This fund will provide a safety net during challenging times and help you avoid resorting to credit cards or loans.

Stay Disciplined with Credit Cards: If you choose to use credit cards, be disciplined in paying off the full balance each month. Avoid carrying a credit card balance as it can quickly accumulate high-interest debt. Responsible credit card use can help build a positive credit history and improve your credit score.

Involve Your Family: If you have a family, involve them in the budgeting process. Discuss financial goals together and make decisions as a team. Having everyone on board and understanding the importance of sticking to the budget creates a supportive and accountable environment.

Review and Adjust Regularly: Life circumstances change, and your budget should adapt accordingly. Regularly review your budget and make adjustments as needed. A flexible budget allows you to accommodate unexpected changes while staying aligned with your long-term financial objectives.

Seek Support and Accountability: Share your budgeting goals with friends, family, or a financial advisor. Having a support system and someone to hold you accountable can help you stay motivated and committed to your budgeting efforts.

In conclusion, sticking to your budget requires discipline, mindfulness, and a clear understanding of your financial priorities. By setting realistic goals, tracking expenses diligently, prioritizing spending, and avoiding impulsive decisions, you can maintain control over your finances and work towards your financial goals. Remember that budgeting is a dynamic process, and it's okay to make adjustments as needed. Stay persistent and patient, and you'll reap the rewards of financial security and success.

Chapter 3: Building an Emergency Fund and Managing Debt

3.1 Establishing an Emergency Fund

In the pursuit of financial freedom and living debt-free, one of the most crucial steps you can take is to establish an emergency fund. An emergency fund acts as a financial safety net, providing you with a cushion against unexpected expenses and unforeseen circumstances. It serves as a crucial component of your overall financial plan, offering peace of mind and stability during challenging times.

The purpose of an emergency fund is to cover essential living expenses when faced with unexpected events, such as medical emergencies, job loss, car repairs, or major home repairs. Without a sufficient emergency fund, you may be forced to rely on credit cards, loans, or other forms of debt to meet these sudden financial demands, leading to potential debt accumulation and financial strain.

When establishing an emergency fund, the first step is to determine the ideal amount you need to set aside. A commonly recommended target is to have three to six months' worth of living expenses saved. However, this number may vary based on individual circumstances, such as job stability, family size, and any other potential sources of financial support.

To calculate your desired emergency fund amount, review your monthly expenses, including rent or mortgage payments, utilities, groceries, insurance premiums, and other essential living costs. Multiply this figure by the number of months you wish to cover with your emergency fund. Remember to consider any additional expenses specific to your situation, such as medical costs or childcare.

Building an emergency fund takes time and discipline. It is best to start by setting smaller, achievable milestones and gradually work towards your ultimate target. Consider automating your savings by setting up automatic transfers to a dedicated savings account with each paycheck. Treating your emergency fund as a non-negotiable expense will ensure consistent contributions over time.

As you build your emergency fund, keep it separate from your regular checking account and other savings goals. This separation helps prevent accidental spending and ensures that your emergency fund remains intact for when you truly need it.

When faced with an emergency, access your emergency fund judiciously. Use the funds only for genuine emergencies, not for non-essential expenses or impulse purchases. Consider whether the expense aligns with the purpose of the emergency fund before tapping into it. If you do need to use your emergency fund, make it a priority to replenish it as soon as possible.

An emergency fund is not just a one-time savings goal but a dynamic financial tool that requires ongoing attention and maintenance. Regularly review your expenses and update your emergency fund target to reflect any changes in your financial situation or living expenses.

Building an emergency fund is a crucial foundation for your financial well-being. It not only provides financial security but also alleviates stress and anxiety during uncertain times. With an emergency fund in place, you gain the confidence to navigate through unexpected challenges without jeopardizing your long-term financial goals.

3.2 Understanding Different Types of Debt

Debt is a common financial tool that allows individuals and businesses to access funds for various purposes. While not inherently negative, debt requires responsible management to avoid falling into a cycle of debt and financial hardship. Understanding the different types of debt is essential for making informed financial decisions and working towards a debt-free life.

Consumer Debt: Consumer debt refers to money borrowed to finance personal expenses and purchases. Common forms of consumer debt include credit card debt, personal loans, and payday loans. While consumer debt can provide short-term convenience, it often comes with high-interest rates, making it challenging to repay, especially when left unpaid over extended periods.

Mortgage Debt: Mortgage debt is the debt incurred when purchasing real estate. It involves taking out a loan to buy a home or property and repaying the loan over an extended period, usually 15 to 30 years. Mortgage debt is often considered "good debt" as it allows individuals to build equity and own a valuable asset while enjoying potential tax benefits.

Student Loans: Student loans are debts taken on to finance education expenses. They can come from government programs or private lenders and typically offer lower interest rates than consumer debt. However, excessive student loan debt can burden graduates for many years after completing their education.

Auto Loans: Auto loans are debts used to finance the purchase of a vehicle. Similar to mortgages, auto loans allow individuals to spread the cost of a car over several years. While auto loans can be convenient, they may result in negative equity if the vehicle's value depreciates faster than the loan balance is paid down.

Business Debt: Business debt refers to money borrowed by businesses to finance operations, expansion, or capital investments. It can include bank loans, lines of credit, or bonds. Managing business debt requires careful consideration of the company's cash flow and ability to generate profits.

Payday Loans: Payday loans are short-term, high-interest loans designed to provide quick cash to borrowers. These loans often target individuals in urgent need of money but can trap them in a cycle of debt due to the high fees and interest rates associated with them.

Medical Debt: Medical debt arises when individuals incur expenses related to healthcare services not covered by insurance. Medical debt can become burdensome, especially for those without adequate health insurance coverage.

Tax Debt: Tax debt occurs when individuals or businesses owe unpaid taxes to the government. Failure to address tax debt can lead to penalties and interest charges.

Understanding the different types of debt is crucial for making wise financial decisions. Good debt, such as mortgage debt or student loans, can provide opportunities for growth and wealth-building. However, it is essential to manage these debts responsibly and avoid excessive borrowing.

On the other hand, high-interest consumer debt and payday loans can lead to financial stress and make it challenging to achieve financial goals. Reducing and eliminating consumer debt should be a priority for those seeking to become debt-free.

It is crucial to develop a plan for debt repayment, prioritizing high-interest debts first and using strategies like debt consolidation or refinancing to manage debt more effectively. Creating a budget, tracking expenses, and seeking professional advice if needed can all contribute to a successful debt management plan.

Remember that debt is a financial tool that should be used judiciously. Assess the purpose and terms of any debt before taking it on, and avoid overextending yourself financially. By understanding the different types of debt and managing them responsibly, you can take control of your financial future and work towards a life free from the burden of excessive debt.

3.3 Developing a Debt Repayment Plan

Debt can be a significant obstacle on the path to financial freedom and living debt-free. To regain control over your financial life and work towards a debt-free future, developing a debt repayment plan is essential. A well-structured debt repayment plan can help you tackle your debts strategically, stay focused, and make steady progress towards achieving your financial goals.

Assess Your Debts: Begin by assessing all your debts, including credit card balances, student loans, personal loans, auto loans, and any other outstanding debts. Create a comprehensive list detailing the principal amount owed, the interest rates, minimum monthly payments, and the remaining terms for each debt. This clear overview of your debts will provide the foundation for your repayment plan.

Prioritize High-Interest Debts: High-interest debts, such as credit card debts, can quickly accumulate and become a financial burden. To minimize interest payments and save money in the long run, prioritize paying off high-interest debts first. Allocate more of your available funds towards these debts while making minimum payments on lower-interest debts.

Consider Debt Consolidation: If you have multiple high-interest debts, explore the option of debt consolidation. Debt consolidation involves combining several debts into a single loan with a lower interest rate. Consolidation can make it easier to manage your debts and potentially reduce your monthly payments, making it more feasible to repay the debt over time.

Choose a Repayment Strategy: There are various debt repayment strategies you can consider, such as the snowball method or the avalanche method. The snowball method involves prioritizing the smallest debts first, while the avalanche method focuses on the highest interest debts. Choose the strategy that aligns with your financial situation and motivates you to stay committed.

Set Realistic Repayment Goals: Set achievable repayment goals based on your income, expenses, and financial priorities. Be realistic about how much you can allocate towards debt repayment each month, taking into account other essential expenses and savings goals. Setting realistic goals ensures that you stay on track and avoid setting yourself up for disappointment.

Create a Budget: Develop a budget that includes your debt repayment plan. Allocate a specific amount each month towards debt repayment, and ensure that you stick to this commitment. A budget will help you manage your finances effectively and prevent overspending on non-essential items.

Increase Your Income: Consider ways to increase your income to accelerate your debt repayment. This may involve seeking a higher-paying job, starting a side business, freelancing, or taking on part-time work. The additional income can be directed towards debt repayment, helping you become debt-free faster.

Negotiate with Creditors: In some cases, it may be possible to negotiate with creditors for better repayment terms. If you are facing financial hardship, reach out to your creditors and explain your situation. They may be willing to offer temporary relief or adjust the terms to help you stay on track with your repayment plan.

Stay Motivated and Persistent: Debt repayment can be a challenging and lengthy process. It is essential to stay motivated and persistent throughout your journey. Celebrate every milestone, no matter how small, and remind yourself of the financial freedom and peace of mind that await you at the end of the road.

Seek Professional Advice: If you find it challenging to develop a debt repayment plan or manage your debts effectively, consider seeking advice from a financial advisor or credit counselor. These professionals can provide personalized guidance and support, helping you navigate through challenging financial situations.

3.4 Tips for Avoiding Debt Traps

Avoiding debt traps is crucial for maintaining financial stability and working towards a debt-free life. Debt traps are situations where individuals find themselves overwhelmed by debt, often due to poor financial decisions or unforeseen circumstances. By adopting mindful financial habits and implementing responsible strategies, you can safeguard yourself from falling into debt traps. Here are some tips to help you avoid debt traps:

Create a Realistic Budget: Developing a realistic budget is the foundation of sound financial management. Evaluate your income, expenses, and financial goals to create a budget that aligns with your financial capacity. Be sure to include savings for emergencies and future goals. Stick to your budget diligently, and track your expenses regularly to stay on course.

Live Within Your Means: Avoid the temptation to spend beyond your means. Prioritize needs over wants, and resist impulse purchases. Consider the long-term impact of each expense on your financial well-being. Living within your means allows you to save more and avoid unnecessary debt.

Save for Emergencies: Building an emergency fund is critical for protecting yourself from financial emergencies. Aim to save three to six months' worth of living expenses in an easily accessible account. With an emergency fund in place, you won't have to rely on credit cards or loans when unexpected expenses arise.

Pay Bills on Time: Late payments can lead to penalties, increased interest rates, and a negative impact on your credit score. Paying bills on time is a simple but effective way to maintain a good credit history and avoid unnecessary debt.

Use Credit Wisely: Credit cards can be useful financial tools if used responsibly. Only charge what you can afford to pay off each month and avoid carrying a balance whenever possible. Keep your credit utilization ratio low, as high credit card balances can negatively impact your credit score.

Limit Borrowing: Be cautious when borrowing money, and only take on debt for necessary and well-thought-out purposes. Avoid using payday loans or high-interest loans that can lead to a cycle of debt. Instead, explore alternative options like low-interest personal loans or credit unions.

Resist Peer Pressure: Avoid succumbing to peer pressure and societal expectations to overspend on non-essential items or experiences. Remember that everyone's financial situation is different, and it's essential to prioritize your long-term financial health over short-term indulgences.

Avoid Retail Therapy: Emotional spending can lead to impulsive purchases and buyer's remorse. Instead of turning to retail therapy to cope with stress or emotions, find healthier outlets like exercise, spending time with loved ones, or engaging in hobbies.

Regularly Review Your Finances: Take the time to review your financial situation regularly. Assess your budget, track your expenses, and check your credit report for any errors or suspicious activities. Staying aware of your financial standing empowers you to address potential issues early on.

Seek Professional Advice: If you're facing financial challenges or uncertainty, don't hesitate to seek advice from a financial advisor or credit counselor. These professionals can provide personalized guidance and help you develop a plan to overcome your financial hurdles.

In conclusion, avoiding debt traps is essential for maintaining financial well-being and achieving your long-term financial goals. Adopt responsible financial habits, create a realistic budget, and prioritize saving and living within your means. Use credit wisely and avoid excessive borrowing. Stay mindful of your financial decisions and seek professional advice if needed. By implementing these tips, you can steer clear of debt traps and work towards a more secure and debt-free future. Remember that financial freedom is achievable with discipline, determination, and thoughtful financial planning.

Chapter 4: Mastering the Art of Saving and Investing

4.1 Understanding the Power of Saving

Saving is a fundamental financial practice that empowers individuals to build wealth, achieve financial goals, and secure their future. The power of saving lies in its ability to provide financial security, create opportunities, and foster a sense of control over one's financial life. By understanding and harnessing the benefits of saving, individuals can make significant strides towards financial freedom and living debt-free.

Building Financial Security: One of the primary advantages of saving is the sense of financial security it brings. Having savings allows you to face unexpected expenses and emergencies without resorting to high-interest debt. An adequate emergency fund acts as a safety net, ensuring that you can weather financial storms and avoid the stress of living paycheck to paycheck.

Accomplishing Financial Goals: Saving enables you to work towards specific financial goals, whether it's purchasing a home, funding education, starting a business, or retiring comfortably. By consistently setting aside money for these objectives, you create a roadmap for achieving them, turning dreams into reality.

Capitalizing on Opportunities: Saving puts you in a better position to seize opportunities when they arise. Whether it's investing in a promising venture, taking advantage of a limited-time offer, or making a life-changing decision, having savings gives you the flexibility and resources to act swiftly and confidently.

Reducing Financial Stress: Financial stress is a prevalent issue that can impact overall well-being and relationships. By saving regularly and having a financial buffer, you reduce the anxiety associated with money matters. Financial peace of mind contributes to a happier and healthier life.

Breaking the Cycle of Debt: Saving and debt are interconnected in the sense that saving can help break the cycle of debt. When you have savings to rely on, you're less likely to turn to credit cards or loans to cover expenses, thus avoiding high-interest debt accumulation.

Growing Wealth Over Time: Saving, coupled with investing, has the power to grow wealth over time. The compounding effect of investments allows your money to generate returns, building on itself year after year. Starting early and remaining consistent in your savings and investment efforts can significantly impact your long-term wealth.

Developing Financial Discipline: Saving requires discipline and self-control. By cultivating these qualities, you enhance your ability to make wise financial decisions in other areas of your life. Financial discipline also enables you to resist impulsive spending and stick to your budget and long-term goals.

Navigating Life Transitions: Life is full of transitions, such as job changes, marriage, starting a family, or retirement. Saving provides a buffer during these transitions, making them smoother and less financially challenging. It allows you to adapt to changing circumstances without derailing your financial plans.

Leaving a Legacy: Saving is not only about your financial well-being but also about leaving a legacy for your loved ones. By building wealth and being financially responsible, you can pass on financial knowledge, assets, and opportunities to future generations.

Fostering Financial Independence: Ultimately, saving fosters financial independence. It allows you to rely on your own resources and decisions rather than depending on others or being bound by debt. Financial independence provides the freedom to live life on your terms and pursue your passions and interests.

In conclusion, understanding the power of saving is essential for achieving financial security and working towards a debt-free life. Saving provides financial stability, allows you to achieve your goals, and empowers you to navigate life's challenges with confidence. It reduces financial stress, fosters discipline, and helps you grow wealth over time. By embracing the practice of saving and making it a priority in your financial journey, you can unlock the doors to financial freedom and open up a world of possibilities for your future.

4.2 Exploring Different Investment Options

Investing is a powerful tool for building wealth and achieving financial goals. It allows individuals to put their money to work, generate returns, and grow their assets over time. Exploring different investment options is essential for diversifying your portfolio, managing risk, and maximizing your long-term returns. Here are some common investment options to consider:

Stocks: Stocks represent ownership in a company. When you buy shares of a company's stock, you become a shareholder and have a stake in the company's success. Stock prices fluctuate based on market conditions, company performance, and other factors. Investing in stocks can provide the potential for significant returns, but it also comes with higher risks compared to other investments.

Bonds: Bonds are debt securities issued by governments, municipalities, or corporations. When you buy a bond, you are essentially lending money to the issuer in exchange for regular interest payments and the return of the bond's face value at maturity. Bonds are generally considered less risky than stocks and can provide a steady income stream.

Mutual Funds: Mutual funds pool money from multiple investors to invest in a diversified portfolio of stocks, bonds, or other securities. They are managed by professional portfolio managers. Investing in mutual funds provides diversification and convenience, as the fund manager makes investment decisions on your behalf.

Exchange-Traded Funds (ETFs): ETFs are similar to mutual funds but trade on stock exchanges like individual stocks. They offer diversification and are often passively managed, tracking specific market indices. ETFs can be bought and sold throughout the trading day at market prices.

Real Estate: Real estate investments involve buying properties for rental income or capital appreciation. Real estate can provide a steady stream of rental income and potential tax benefits. However, it requires active management and carries the risk of property value fluctuations.

Retirement Accounts: Retirement accounts like Individual Retirement Accounts (IRAs) and 401(k)s offer tax advantages for long-term retirement savings. Traditional IRAs and 401(k)s offer tax-deferred contributions, while Roth IRAs and Roth 401(k)s provide tax-free withdrawals in retirement.

Certificate of Deposit (CD): CDs are time deposits offered by banks with fixed terms and interest rates. They are low-risk investments, but the funds are locked in until the CD matures. CDs can be suitable for short-term savings or as a part of a conservative investment strategy.

Commodities: Commodities are physical goods like gold, silver, oil, or agricultural products. Investing in commodities can provide diversification and a hedge against inflation. However, commodity prices can be volatile, making it a riskier investment option.

Peer-to-Peer Lending: Peer-to-peer lending platforms connect borrowers with individual investors willing to lend money. Investors earn interest on their loans, while borrowers get access to funding outside of traditional banks. Peer-to-peer lending carries credit risk, and investors should diversify their loans to manage risk.

Art and Collectibles: Investing in art, collectibles, or other tangible assets can provide potential appreciation in value. However, valuing and selling such assets can be challenging, and the market for these investments may be less liquid.

Before investing, consider your risk tolerance, time horizon, and financial goals. Diversifying your investments across various asset classes can help spread risk and enhance potential returns. It's essential to conduct thorough research or seek advice from a financial advisor to make informed investment decisions aligned with your unique circumstances.

Additionally, stay informed about economic trends, market conditions, and the performance of your investments. Regularly review your investment portfolio and rebalance it as needed to maintain your desired asset allocation. Remember that investing is a long-term endeavor, and patience and discipline are key to achieving success in the world of investments.

4.3 Creating a Diversified Investment Portfolio

A diversified investment portfolio is a key strategy for managing risk and maximizing returns in the world of investments. Diversification involves spreading your investments across different asset classes, industries, and geographic regions to reduce exposure to the volatility of any single investment. By creating a diversified investment portfolio, you can enhance the potential for long-term growth while safeguarding against significant losses. Here are some essential considerations when building a diversified investment portfolio:

Asset Allocation: Asset allocation is the process of deciding how to distribute your investments across different asset classes, such as stocks, bonds, real estate, and cash equivalents. The appropriate asset allocation depends on your financial goals, risk tolerance, and investment time horizon. A well-balanced asset allocation aligns with your risk appetite while providing opportunities for growth.

Stocks: Stocks represent ownership in a company and can offer significant growth potential over the long term. However, they are subject to market volatility and carry higher risks compared to other asset classes. When selecting stocks for your portfolio, consider investing in companies of different sizes, industries, and geographical regions to diversify your exposure.

Bonds: Bonds are debt securities that offer fixed interest payments and return of principal at maturity. They are generally considered less risky than stocks and provide a stable income stream. Include a mix of government, corporate, and municipal bonds with varying maturities to diversify your bond investments.

Real Estate: Real estate investments can add diversification to your portfolio and provide a hedge against inflation. Consider investing in real estate investment trusts (REITs) or real estate crowdfunding platforms to gain exposure to the real estate market without the need to manage physical properties.

Cash Equivalents: Cash equivalents, such as money market funds and short-term Treasury bills, provide liquidity and act as a safe haven during market downturns. They can be an essential component of a diversified portfolio, offering stability during volatile market conditions.

International Investments: Including international investments in your portfolio provides exposure to foreign markets and can offer diversification benefits. Consider investing in international stocks and bonds to capitalize on global economic growth opportunities.

Exchange-Traded Funds (ETFs): ETFs are a convenient way to achieve diversification within each asset class. They track market indices and offer exposure to a broad range of stocks, bonds, or commodities. Consider using ETFs to access specific sectors or markets while maintaining diversification.

Rebalancing: Regularly review and rebalance your investment portfolio to maintain your desired asset allocation. Market fluctuations can cause your portfolio to drift away from your original allocation. Rebalancing involves selling some assets that have outperformed and reinvesting in assets that may be undervalued.

Risk Management: Diversification is a risk management strategy that can protect your portfolio from severe losses. While it may not eliminate all risk, it can help reduce the impact of negative market movements on your overall investments.

Long-Term Perspective: A diversified investment portfolio is designed for the long term. Avoid making impulsive decisions based on short-term market fluctuations. Stay focused on your financial goals and the well-structured plan you have put in place.

Remember that diversification does not guarantee profits or protect against all losses, but it is an essential strategy for mitigating risk and increasing the potential for long-term growth. Building a diversified investment portfolio requires careful consideration of your financial objectives, risk tolerance, and investment time horizon. As your circumstances change, revisit and adjust your portfolio to ensure it remains aligned with your goals and current market conditions. By maintaining a disciplined and diversified approach to investing, you can set yourself on the path to a more secure financial future.

4.4 Managing Risks and Market Volatility

Investing in financial markets comes with inherent risks and uncertainties. Market volatility, economic downturns, and unexpected events can significantly impact investment performance. Managing these risks is essential for protecting your investment portfolio and achieving long-term financial success. Here are some strategies to help you manage risks and navigate market volatility:

Diversification: As mentioned earlier, diversification is a fundamental risk management strategy. By spreading your investments across different asset classes, industries, and geographical regions, you reduce the impact of adverse market movements on your overall portfolio. Diversification helps mitigate the risk of any single investment significantly affecting your entire portfolio.

Risk Tolerance Assessment: Understand your risk tolerance before making investment decisions. Risk tolerance refers to your ability and willingness to withstand fluctuations in the value of your investments. Assess your financial goals, investment time horizon, and emotional capacity to handle market volatility. Align your investments with your risk tolerance to avoid making hasty decisions during turbulent market conditions.

Dollar-Cost Averaging: Dollar-cost averaging involves investing a fixed amount of money at regular intervals, regardless of market conditions. This strategy allows you to buy more shares when prices are low and fewer shares when prices are high. Dollar-cost averaging helps reduce the impact of market volatility on your investment returns and provides discipline in building your portfolio over time.

Avoid Emotional Decisions: Emotional decisions can lead to costly mistakes in investing. Fear and panic during market downturns may drive you to sell investments at the wrong time. Conversely, euphoria during bull markets can lead to overconfidence and excessive risk-taking. Stay focused on your long-term goals and avoid making impulsive decisions based on short-term market movements.

Regular Portfolio Review: Conduct regular reviews of your investment portfolio to ensure it remains aligned with your financial goals and risk tolerance. As your circumstances change, you may need to rebalance your portfolio or make adjustments to stay on track. A well-structured and regularly reviewed portfolio can better withstand market volatility.

Long-Term Investment Horizon: Adopt a long-term investment horizon and avoid making short-term bets based on speculation or market timing. Time in the market is generally more important than timing the market. Staying invested over the long term allows you to benefit from compounding returns and potentially overcome short-term market fluctuations.

Hedging Strategies: Consider implementing hedging strategies to protect your portfolio from potential downside risks. Hedging involves using financial instruments like options or futures to offset potential losses in your investments. While hedging can provide some protection, it may also limit your potential gains.

Asset Allocation Rebalancing: Rebalancing your portfolio involves adjusting your asset allocation back to your target percentages. Regular rebalancing ensures that your portfolio remains diversified and reduces exposure to overvalued or underperforming assets. Rebalancing is a disciplined approach to managing risk and maintaining your desired risk profile.

Education and Professional Advice: Educate yourself about investing and financial markets to make informed decisions. Knowledge about different asset classes, investment vehicles, and economic trends can empower you to navigate market volatility confidently. If needed, seek advice from a financial advisor who understands your financial goals and risk tolerance.

Stay Informed and Prepared: Stay informed about market developments, economic indicators, and geopolitical events that may affect your investments. Being prepared and aware of potential risks can help you respond appropriately to changing market conditions.

In conclusion, managing risks and market volatility is a crucial aspect of successful investing. Diversification, risk tolerance assessment, dollar-cost averaging, and avoiding emotional decisions are essential strategies to protect your investments. Regular portfolio reviews, a long-term investment horizon, and hedging strategies can further enhance risk management. Educating yourself about investing and seeking professional advice can help you navigate market uncertainties with confidence. Remember that investing involves risks, but with a well-structured approach and disciplined decision-making, you can increase your chances of achieving your financial goals over the long term.

Chapter 5: Navigating Major Financial Decisions

5.1 Buying vs. Renting: Making the Right Choice

The decision to buy or rent a home is one of the most significant financial choices individuals face. Both options come with their own set of advantages and drawbacks, and making the right choice depends on various factors, including your financial situation, lifestyle, and long-term goals. Let's explore the considerations for buying and renting to help you make an informed decision that aligns with your needs.

Buying a Home:

Long-Term Investment: Purchasing a home is often considered a long-term investment. Over time, real estate properties can appreciate in value, providing homeowners with potential equity and an asset that can contribute to their overall wealth.

Building Equity: With each mortgage payment, homeowners build equity in their property. Equity represents the difference between the home's value and the remaining mortgage balance. As you build equity, you gain ownership in the property, which can be tapped into through home equity loans or by selling the property.

Stability and Control: Homeownership offers stability and control over your living environment. You have the freedom to customize and renovate your home as you wish, providing a sense of permanence and personalization.

Tax Benefits: Homeowners may benefit from tax deductions on mortgage interest and property taxes, reducing their taxable income. These tax benefits can make homeownership more financially appealing.

Predictable Housing Costs: With a fixed-rate mortgage, homeowners enjoy predictable housing costs over the long term. Unlike renting, where rents can increase annually, mortgage payments remain stable, providing financial certainty.

Responsibility for Maintenance: Homeownership comes with the responsibility of maintaining the property. Homeowners must budget for repairs, maintenance, and unexpected expenses related to the home.

Initial Costs: Buying a home requires a significant upfront investment, including a down payment, closing costs, and other fees. Saving for a down payment can be challenging, especially for first-time homebuyers.

Renting a Home:

Flexibility and Mobility: Renting offers flexibility, making it an attractive choice for those with uncertain job situations or who prefer the freedom to move without being tied to a property.

Lower Initial Costs: Renting typically requires a smaller upfront investment compared to buying. Renters are responsible for a security deposit and often the first month's rent, making it more accessible for those with limited savings.

Limited Responsibility for Maintenance: Renters are generally not responsible for major repairs or maintenance. Landlords are responsible for addressing structural issues and ensuring the property's habitability.

Diversifying Investments: Renters can invest their savings in other assets rather than tying them up in a home. This approach allows for greater diversification of investments, potentially yielding higher returns.

Protection from Market Fluctuations: Renters are shielded from fluctuations in the real estate market. Changes in property values and interest rates do not directly impact renters, providing a level of financial security.

Limited Control over Living Space: Renters have less control over their living space. They may be restricted from making significant changes or customizations to the property without the landlord's permission.

Rent Increases: Renters face the risk of rent increases at the end of each lease term. Frequent increases can make budgeting for housing costs more challenging in the long run.

Making the Right Choice:

When deciding between buying and renting, consider your financial stability, lifestyle preferences, and long-term goals. Buying a home can be a wise investment if you plan to stay in the property for several years and are financially prepared for the initial costs and ongoing responsibilities. Homeownership offers stability, equity-building potential, and tax benefits.

On the other hand, renting may be a better option if you prefer flexibility, mobility, and a lower upfront investment. Renting allows you to allocate your savings towards other investments or financial goals. If you are uncertain about your future plans or prefer to delegate maintenance responsibilities to the landlord, renting might be the more suitable choice.

It's important to assess your current financial situation, including your credit score, income stability, and debt-to-income ratio, before making a decision. Consider consulting with a financial advisor or a real estate professional to evaluate your options based on your individual circumstances.

5.2 Understanding Mortgages and Homeownership

Mortgages play a crucial role in the journey to homeownership, enabling individuals and families to purchase properties they might not be able to afford outright. Understanding how mortgages work is essential for anyone considering buying a home, as it involves complex financial decisions that can have a significant impact on one's long-term financial health. Let's delve into the key aspects of mortgages and homeownership to gain a comprehensive understanding of this important financial process.

What is a Mortgage?

A mortgage is a loan provided by a lender, usually a bank or a financial institution, to help individuals or families purchase real estate. The property being purchased serves as collateral for the loan, meaning that if the borrower fails to make mortgage payments, the lender has the right to foreclose on the property to recover their investment. Mortgages typically have a fixed or adjustable interest rate and a specified term, commonly ranging from 15 to 30 years.

Down Payment and Loan-to-Value Ratio:

When applying for a mortgage, the borrower is required to make a down payment, which is a percentage of the property's purchase price. The down payment is an upfront payment towards the home, and the remaining amount is covered by the mortgage loan. The loan-to-value (LTV) ratio represents the percentage of the home's value that is financed through the mortgage. For example, if a home is purchased for

$200,000, and the borrower makes a $40,000 (20%) down payment, the loan-to-value ratio is 80%.

Types of Mortgages:

There are various types of mortgages available to borrowers, each with its own features and benefits. Some common types include:

Fixed-Rate Mortgage: In a fixed-rate mortgage, the interest rate remains constant throughout the loan term. This provides borrowers with predictability and stability in their monthly mortgage payments.

Adjustable-Rate Mortgage (ARM): An adjustable-rate mortgage comes with an initial fixed-rate period, followed by periodic adjustments to the interest rate based on market conditions. ARMs can offer lower initial rates but carry the risk of rate fluctuations.

Government-Backed Mortgages: Government-backed mortgages, such as FHA, VA, and USDA loans, are insured or guaranteed by government agencies. These loans often come with more flexible qualification requirements and lower down payment options.

Jumbo Loans: Jumbo loans are designed for high-priced properties that exceed the conforming loan limits set by Fannie Mae and Freddie Mac. Jumbo loans typically require higher credit scores and down payment amounts.

The Homebuying Process:

The homebuying process involves several steps, from finding the right property to closing the deal. Key stages include:

Pre-Approval: Before starting the search for a home, prospective buyers should get pre-approved for a mortgage. This process involves providing financial information to the lender, who then determines the maximum loan amount the buyer qualifies for.

House Hunting: Once pre-approved, the home search begins. Buyers work with real estate agents, visit properties, and evaluate potential options based on their preferences and budget.

Making an Offer: When buyers find a suitable property, they make an offer to the seller. The offer includes the proposed purchase price and any contingencies or conditions.

Underwriting and Closing: After the seller accepts the offer, the mortgage goes through underwriting, where the lender verifies the borrower's financial information and the property's value. Once approved, the closing process takes place, and ownership of the property is transferred to the buyer.

Responsibilities of Homeownership:

Owning a home comes with financial and maintenance responsibilities. Homeowners must make timely mortgage payments, pay property taxes, and maintain homeowner's insurance. Additionally, homeowners are responsible for property maintenance and repairs.

Benefits of Homeownership:

Homeownership offers several benefits:

Equity Building: As homeowners make mortgage payments, they build equity in the property. Equity represents the difference between the home's value and the remaining mortgage balance.

Tax Benefits: Homeowners may benefit from tax deductions on mortgage interest and property taxes, which can reduce their taxable income.

Stability and Personalization: Homeownership provides stability and the freedom to customize and personalize the living space according to the homeowner's preferences.

Challenges of Homeownership:

While homeownership offers numerous advantages, it also presents challenges:

Initial Costs: The upfront costs of buying a home, including the down payment, closing costs, and other fees, can be significant.

Financial Commitment: Owning a home is a long-term financial commitment that requires steady income and financial stability to manage mortgage payments and related expenses.

Property Maintenance: Homeowners are responsible for ongoing property maintenance and repairs, which can add to the overall cost of homeownership.

In conclusion, understanding mortgages and homeownership is vital for anyone considering buying a home. Mortgages provide a pathway to homeownership by enabling individuals and families to finance the purchase of real estate. Different types of mortgages offer various features and benefits, catering to diverse financial situations and preferences. The homebuying process involves multiple stages, from pre-approval to closing, and comes with financial and maintenance responsibilities. While homeownership offers numerous advantages, potential buyers must weigh the costs and commitments associated with owning a home. Ultimately, making an informed decision about homeownership ensures a solid foundation for a stable and fulfilling financial future.

5.3 Planning for Retirement and Long-Term Savings

Planning for retirement and long-term savings is a critical aspect of financial wellbeing. It involves setting financial goals, making informed investment decisions, and diligently saving for the future. With increasing life expectancies and potential economic uncertainties, it is essential to start planning for retirement early to ensure a comfortable and secure future. Let's explore the key components of retirement planning and long-term savings to help you prepare for a financially sound tomorrow.

Setting Retirement Goals: The first step in retirement planning is to define your retirement goals. Consider factors such as the age you wish to retire, the lifestyle you envision, and the activities you want to pursue during retirement. Having clear goals will help you determine the amount of money you need to save and invest to achieve your retirement dreams.

Understanding Retirement Accounts: Familiarize yourself with retirement accounts, such as Individual Retirement Accounts (IRAs) and 401(k)s. These accounts offer tax advantages, allowing your savings to grow tax-free or tax-deferred until retirement. Take advantage of employer-sponsored retirement plans if available, as they often come with matching contributions, which can significantly boost your savings.

Calculating Retirement Needs: Estimating your retirement needs involves evaluating your expected expenses during retirement, including housing, healthcare, travel, and daily living costs. Consider inflation and potential healthcare expenses, as these can significantly impact your retirement budget. Online retirement calculators and financial advisors can help you assess your retirement needs based on your current financial situation and goals.

Diversifying Retirement Investments: Diversification is crucial when investing for retirement. Consider a mix of stocks, bonds, and other investment vehicles to balance risk and potential returns. As retirement approaches, consider gradually shifting towards more conservative investments to protect your savings from market volatility.

Consistent Savings: Consistency is key to successful retirement planning. Make saving for retirement a regular habit, and contribute to your retirement accounts consistently. Automated contributions from your paycheck or bank account can help ensure that you stay on track with your savings goals.

Emergency Fund: Building an emergency fund is essential before prioritizing long-term savings. An emergency fund provides a financial buffer to cover unexpected expenses, preventing you from dipping into your retirement savings during challenging times.

Long-Term Savings Goals: In addition to retirement, consider other long-term savings goals, such as funding your children's education, buying a home, or starting a business. Allocate a portion of your savings towards these goals, but not at the expense of neglecting your retirement savings.

Healthcare and Insurance: Health expenses can be significant during retirement. Evaluate healthcare options, including Medicare and supplemental insurance plans. Ensuring adequate coverage can protect your retirement savings from unforeseen medical costs.

Reevaluate and Adjust: Life circumstances change, and it's essential to regularly reevaluate your retirement plan. Major life events, such as marriage, having children, or a career change, may impact your financial goals and savings strategies. Be prepared to adjust your retirement plan accordingly.

Seek Professional Advice: Retirement planning can be complex, and seeking advice from a financial advisor can provide valuable insights and personalized guidance. A financial advisor can help you create a comprehensive retirement plan based on your unique circumstances and financial objectives.

In conclusion, planning for retirement and long-term savings is a vital aspect of securing your financial future. Start early, set clear retirement goals, and take advantage of retirement accounts and employer-sponsored plans. Diversify your investments, save consistently, and build an emergency fund to protect your retirement savings. Consider other long-term savings goals while prioritizing retirement planning. Regularly reassess your retirement plan, and seek professional advice to make informed decisions. With careful planning and disciplined financial management, you can pave the way for a comfortable and fulfilling retirement, ensuring that your golden years are spent stress-free and enjoying the fruits of your labor.

5.4 Making Informed Insurance Choices

Insurance plays a crucial role in managing financial risk and protecting oneself, family, and assets from unforeseen events. It provides a safety net that can help mitigate the financial impact of accidents, illnesses, property damage, and other unexpected situations. However, making informed insurance choices can be challenging, given the vast array of insurance products and providers available. Understanding your insurance needs, evaluating coverage options, and comparing policies can ensure that you choose the right insurance coverage for your specific circumstances.

Assessing Insurance Needs: The first step in making informed insurance choices is to assess your insurance needs. Consider the various aspects of your life that need protection, such as health, life, property, and liability. Evaluate your risk tolerance and financial situation to determine the level of coverage required in each area.

Health Insurance: Health insurance is a fundamental aspect of financial protection. It covers medical expenses, doctor visits, hospitalization, and prescription medications. Choose a health insurance plan that best suits your medical needs and budget, and ensure that it includes coverage for essential services and any pre-existing conditions.

Life Insurance: Life insurance provides financial protection for your loved ones in the event of your passing. There are different types of life insurance, such as term life and whole life insurance. Consider your family's financial needs and future goals when choosing the appropriate life insurance coverage.

Auto Insurance: Auto insurance is mandatory in most places and provides coverage for damages and injuries resulting from accidents involving your vehicle. Choose auto insurance that complies with local regulations and adequately protects you and your vehicle.

Homeowners or Renters Insurance: Homeowners and renters insurance protects your home or personal belongings from theft, damage, or disasters. Evaluate your property's value and the potential risks to determine the appropriate coverage for your needs.

Disability Insurance: Disability insurance provides income protection in case you are unable to work due to a disabling illness or injury. Assess your financial responsibilities and the need for replacement income to choose suitable disability insurance coverage.

Long-Term Care Insurance: Long-term care insurance covers the costs of extended care services, such as nursing home care or home health care, in case of a chronic illness or disability. Consider your family's medical history and the potential need for long-term care to determine if this insurance is necessary.

Liability Insurance: Liability insurance provides protection in case you are legally responsible for injuries to others or damage to their property. Liability coverage is essential for protecting your assets from potential lawsuits.

Compare Policies and Providers: Once you have assessed your insurance needs, compare policies and providers. Obtain quotes from multiple insurance companies to evaluate coverage options, premiums, deductibles, and customer reviews. Look for reputable insurance companies with a track record of excellent customer service and timely claims processing.

Review and Update Regularly: Insurance needs can change over time due to life events, such as marriage, the birth of a child, or major purchases. Regularly review your insurance coverage to ensure it remains adequate and up-to-date with your changing circumstances.

In conclusion, making informed insurance choices is essential for protecting yourself, your family, and your assets from unexpected financial burdens. Assess your insurance needs carefully, considering health, life, property, and liability aspects. Research and compare policies and providers to find the best coverage options that align with your financial situation and risk tolerance. Regularly review your insurance coverage to ensure it remains appropriate for your changing needs. By taking a proactive and informed approach to insurance, you can achieve peace of mind and safeguard your financial well-being.

Chapter 6: Achieving Long-Term Financial Freedom

6.1 Setting Long-Term Financial Goals

Setting long-term financial goals is an essential step in achieving financial success and building a secure future. Long-term financial goals are aspirations that span several years or even decades, helping individuals and families plan for major life events, such as retirement, homeownership, education, or starting a business. These goals provide direction and motivation, guiding financial decisions and shaping the path towards financial independence. Let's explore the process of setting long-term financial goals and the significance of having a well-defined financial roadmap.

Define Your Vision: The first step in setting long-term financial goals is to define your vision for the future. Envision what you want your life to look like in the next five, ten, or twenty years. Consider your dreams, aspirations, and the lifestyle you desire. Having a clear vision will give you a sense of purpose and direction as you embark on your financial journey.

Set Specific Goals: Long-term financial goals should be specific and measurable. Avoid vague goals like "become financially secure." Instead, set specific targets, such as "retire at age 65 with a nest egg of $1 million" or "save for a down payment of $50,000 for a home within five years." Specific goals provide clarity and enable you to track your progress effectively.

Consider Different Aspects: Long-term financial goals cover various aspects of life, including retirement, education, homeownership, travel, and philanthropy. Evaluate each area and prioritize the goals that align with your values and aspirations. Balancing these goals will help you create a comprehensive and well-rounded financial plan.

Create Realistic Timeframes: Setting realistic timeframes for achieving your goals is crucial. Consider your current financial situation, income, expenses, and potential life events. Be mindful of factors that can impact your financial journey, such as inflation and market fluctuations. While it's important to set ambitious goals, be practical in your approach.

Break Down Goals into Milestones: Long-term financial goals can seem overwhelming, especially if they require significant resources or time. Break down each goal into smaller, manageable milestones. Celebrate your achievements at each milestone, as it will motivate you to stay focused and committed to your financial plan.

Quantify Financial Requirements: Determine the financial requirements for each goal. Assess how much money you need to save, invest, or allocate to achieve your goals. Consider consulting with a financial advisor to gain insights into investment strategies and financial planning that align with your objectives.

Regularly Review and Adjust: Life is dynamic, and circumstances can change over time. Regularly review your long-term financial goals and assess your progress. Be prepared to adjust your goals and financial plan to accommodate changes in your life, such as marriage, children, career advancements, or economic conditions.

Involve Family Members: If you have family members or dependents, involve them in the goal-setting process. Discuss financial goals as a family and ensure that everyone is aligned with the vision and contributes to the plan. Family support can strengthen your financial journey and lead to shared accomplishments.

Focus on Financial Education: Enhance your financial knowledge and skills to make well-informed decisions. Attend workshops, read books, and seek guidance from financial experts. Being financially literate empowers you to navigate the complexities of personal finance and investments more effectively.

Cultivate Discipline and Patience: Achieving long-term financial goals requires discipline and patience. Stay committed to your plan, even during challenging times. Avoid impulsive financial decisions and stick to your budget and investment strategy. Over time, discipline and patience will yield significant results.

In conclusion, setting long-term financial goals is a vital step in securing your financial future and realizing your aspirations. Define your vision, set specific goals, and consider different aspects of life that you want to plan for. Create realistic timeframes and break down goals into manageable milestones. Regularly review and adjust your financial plan as circumstances change. Involve family members and invest in financial education to make informed decisions. Cultivate discipline and patience to stay on track with your financial journey. Remember that achieving long-term financial goals is a gradual process, and consistent effort will lead to remarkable financial accomplishments and a more fulfilling life.

6.2 Strategies for Increasing Income

Increasing income is a goal shared by many individuals seeking financial stability and opportunities for a better quality of life. A higher income can provide more significant financial security, open doors for achieving long-term goals, and improve overall well-being. While there are no overnight solutions for increasing income, there are various strategies and approaches that individuals can adopt to boost their earnings. Let's explore some effective strategies for increasing income and achieving greater financial prosperity.

Skill Development and Education: Investing in skill development and education can significantly enhance earning potential. Acquiring new skills or furthering your education can make you more valuable to employers or open up opportunities for career advancement. Continuous learning and professional development can set you apart from your peers and lead to higher-paying positions.

Negotiation and Advocacy: Effective negotiation is a powerful tool for increasing income. When applying for a new job or seeking a raise, negotiate confidently and advocate for your worth. Conduct research to understand salary benchmarks for your industry and position, and use this information to support your negotiation efforts.

Side Hustles and Freelancing: In today's gig economy, side hustles and freelancing offer excellent opportunities to supplement your primary income. Utilize your skills or hobbies to offer services or products on platforms like Upwork, Fiverr, or Etsy. A successful side hustle can generate additional income and potentially grow into a full-time venture.

Start a Business: Entrepreneurship presents a chance to take control of your income. Launching a business allows you to pursue your passion and potentially earn more than traditional employment. While starting a business requires effort and capital, the rewards can be substantial in the long run.

Seek Career Advancement: Climbing the corporate ladder can lead to increased income and better benefits. Demonstrate your value to your employer by consistently delivering excellent results, taking on additional responsibilities, and seeking opportunities for growth within the organization.

Invest in Income-Generating Assets: Investing in income-generating assets, such as stocks, real estate, or dividend-paying securities, can create passive income streams. Over time, your investments can grow and generate returns that supplement your earned income.

Renting Out Property: If you own property, consider renting it out as a source of additional income. Whether it's a spare room, a vacation home, or an investment property, rental income can contribute significantly to your overall earnings.

Build an Online Presence: In today's digital age, having a strong online presence can lead to various income opportunities. Create a blog, YouTube channel, or social media following, and monetize it through advertising, sponsorships, or affiliate marketing.

Pursue High-Demand Professions: Certain professions and industries offer higher income potential due to increased demand for specialized skills. Careers in technology, healthcare, finance, and engineering are often associated with competitive salaries.

Network and Leverage Connections: Networking can lead to new job opportunities, business partnerships, or client referrals. Attend industry events, join professional associations, and build genuine relationships that can help you increase your income through various avenues.

Enhance Sales Skills: Sales professionals often have the potential to earn commissions and bonuses based on performance. Even if you're not in a sales role, enhancing your sales skills can help you negotiate better deals and close higher-paying opportunities.

Embrace a Growth Mindset: Adopting a growth mindset encourages continuous learning and self-improvement. Embrace challenges and view failures as opportunities for growth. With a growth mindset, you'll be more likely to seek out new ways to increase your income.

In conclusion, increasing income requires a combination of effort, dedication, and strategic planning. Investing in skill development and education, negotiating confidently, and seeking career advancement are effective ways to boost earnings. Leveraging side hustles, starting a business, and investing in income-generating assets can create additional streams of income. Building an online presence, renting out property, and pursuing high-demand professions are other avenues to explore. Networking, enhancing sales skills, and embracing a growth mindset can further propel your income growth. Remember that increasing income is a gradual process, and consistent efforts can lead to significant financial rewards and a more prosperous future.

6.3 Reviewing and Adjusting Your Financial Plan

Creating a financial plan is a crucial step in achieving your financial goals and securing your future. However, a financial plan is not a static document; it requires regular review and adjustment to remain relevant and effective. Life is dynamic, and various factors, such as changes in income, expenses, market conditions, and personal circumstances, can influence your financial journey. Reviewing and adjusting your financial plan is essential to ensure that it continues to align with your objectives and adapts to the ever-changing financial landscape. Let's explore the importance of reviewing your financial plan and the key steps involved in making necessary adjustments.

The Importance of Reviewing Your Financial Plan:

Tracking Progress: Regularly reviewing your financial plan allows you to track your progress toward your goals. By assessing your achievements and setbacks, you can make informed decisions on how to stay on course or make necessary changes.

Identifying Changes: Life events, such as marriage, having children, changing jobs, or unexpected expenses, can impact your financial situation. Reviewing your financial plan helps identify changes that may require adjustments to your strategies.

Adapting to Market Conditions: Economic and market conditions can fluctuate, affecting your investments and overall financial well-being. A financial plan review enables you to adapt to these changes and make informed investment decisions.

Optimizing Tax Strategies: Tax laws and regulations may change over time, affecting your tax planning. Regular reviews can help you optimize your tax strategies to minimize tax liability and maximize savings.

Enhancing Efficiency: As you progress in your financial journey, you may discover new opportunities to enhance the efficiency of your financial plan. Reviewing your plan allows you to capitalize on these opportunities.

Steps for Reviewing and Adjusting Your Financial Plan:

Set a Review Schedule: Establish a regular schedule for reviewing your financial plan. Depending on your circumstances, an annual review may be sufficient, while others may benefit from more frequent reviews.

Gather Updated Information: Before conducting a review, gather all relevant financial information, including income, expenses, assets, debts, and investment statements. Ensure you have accurate and current data to base your decisions on.

Assess Progress Toward Goals: Evaluate your progress toward each financial goal. Identify any goals that have been achieved or are within reach and those that may require adjustments or additional efforts.

Analyze Changes in Circumstances: Consider any changes in your life circumstances, such as family dynamics, employment status, health, or lifestyle. These changes may impact your financial priorities and risk tolerance.

Review Investment Performance: Examine the performance of your investments and assess whether they are meeting your expectations. Rebalance your investment portfolio if necessary to maintain the desired asset allocation.

Evaluate Insurance Coverage: Review your insurance policies to ensure they provide adequate coverage for your current needs. Adjust coverage as necessary based on changes in family size, health, or other significant factors.

Check Retirement Readiness: Assess your retirement savings and determine if you are on track to meet your retirement goals. Adjust your retirement contributions if needed to achieve your desired retirement age and income.

Analyze Debt Management: Review your debt situation and evaluate the progress you've made in reducing debt. Consider strategies for accelerating debt repayment or refinancing to save on interest.

Revisit Budget and Spending: Analyze your spending habits and assess if you are sticking to your budget. Identify areas where you can reduce expenses or reallocate funds toward more critical financial goals.

Consult with Financial Advisor: Consider consulting with a financial advisor during the review process. A professional can provide objective insights, personalized guidance, and expertise in financial planning and investment management.

Adjust Financial Strategies: Based on the outcomes of your review, make necessary adjustments to your financial strategies and action plans. Be proactive in aligning your financial plan with your current priorities and goals.

Communicate with Family Members: If you have family members or dependents, involve them in the review process. Communicate any changes to your financial plan that may affect them and ensure everyone is on the same page.

In conclusion, reviewing and adjusting your financial plan is a vital practice for achieving long-term financial success. Regular reviews allow you to track progress, identify changes, and adapt to market conditions and life events. Assess your progress toward goals, analyze changes in circumstances, and evaluate investment performance and insurance coverage. Revisit your budget, retirement readiness, debt management, and overall financial strategies. Consider consulting with a financial advisor for expert guidance. Making necessary adjustments to your financial plan ensures that it remains relevant, effective, and aligned with your evolving financial aspirations and life goals. Remember that financial planning is an ongoing journey, and regular reviews and adjustments are key to staying on course and achieving a financially secure and fulfilling future.

6.4 Embracing a Debt-Free Lifestyle

Living a debt-free lifestyle is a liberating and empowering financial choice that can lead to greater financial security and peace of mind. In today's consumer-driven society, debt has become a common part of life, whether it's credit card debt, student loans, car loans, or mortgages. However, being burdened by debt can limit financial opportunities, increase stress, and delay progress towards long-term goals. Embracing a debt-free lifestyle involves making intentional decisions, adopting smart financial practices, and prioritizing financial freedom. Let's explore the significance of living debt-free and the steps you can take to achieve this financially rewarding lifestyle.

The Significance of Living Debt-Free:

Financial Freedom: Living without debt provides a sense of financial freedom and independence. It allows you to allocate your income towards achieving your goals, rather than servicing debt payments.

Reduced Stress: Debt can cause stress and anxiety, especially when facing high-interest rates or struggling to make monthly payments. Eliminating debt can lead to a more peaceful and mentally healthy life.

Improved Saving and Investing: Without the burden of debt, you can redirect funds towards saving and investing. This can accelerate wealth-building and provide a more secure financial future.

Flexibility in Life Choices: Being debt-free gives you greater flexibility in making life choices. Whether it's pursuing a new career, starting a business, or taking time off for personal development, you have more options without the constraint of debt.

Enhanced Creditworthiness: While living debt-free may mean having less credit, it can positively impact your credit score and creditworthiness. Responsible credit management without excessive debt can make you a more attractive borrower.

Steps to Embrace a Debt-Free Lifestyle:

Assess Your Debt: Begin by assessing your current debt situation. Make a list of all your debts, including outstanding balances, interest rates, and minimum monthly payments. Understanding the full scope of your debt is the first step towards tackling it.

Create a Budget: Establish a realistic budget that outlines your income and expenses. Prioritize essentials and allocate funds towards debt repayment and savings. A well-planned budget will help you live within your means and avoid unnecessary spending.

Develop a Debt Repayment Plan: Once you have a budget, devise a debt repayment plan. There are two common approaches to debt repayment: the debt snowball method and the debt avalanche method. The snowball method involves paying off the smallest debts first to build momentum, while the avalanche method focuses on tackling debts with the highest interest rates first.

Avoid New Debt: Commit to avoiding new debt while you work towards becoming debt-free. Put a hold on credit card spending and only use credit when absolutely necessary. Prioritize cash transactions to prevent accumulating new debt.

Increase Income: Consider increasing your income through side hustles, freelancing, or seeking higher-paying job opportunities. The extra income can be used to accelerate debt repayment and achieve financial goals faster.

Downsize and Simplify: Evaluate your lifestyle and consider downsizing or simplifying to reduce expenses. Cutting unnecessary costs can free up funds to pay off debt and improve your financial position.

Build an Emergency Fund: Creating an emergency fund is crucial for avoiding new debt during unexpected situations. Having a safety net of three to six months' worth of living expenses can protect you from relying on credit during emergencies.

Seek Professional Advice: If you find it challenging to manage your debt, seek advice from a financial counselor or debt specialist. They can provide personalized guidance and support in developing a debt repayment strategy.

Celebrate Milestones: Celebrate your debt repayment milestones along the way. Recognize your progress and use these victories as motivation to continue your debt-free journey.

Cultivate Financial Mindfulness: Embrace financial mindfulness by being intentional with your spending and savings habits. Practice gratitude for what you have and focus on what truly matters to you.

In conclusion, embracing a debt-free lifestyle is a rewarding financial choice that can lead to greater freedom, reduced stress, and improved financial well-being. Assess your debt situation, create a budget, and develop a debt repayment plan. Avoid new debt, increase your income, and downsize where possible to accelerate your progress. Build an emergency fund to protect against new debt during unexpected events. Seek professional advice if needed, and celebrate your milestones along the way. Cultivate financial mindfulness and embrace the journey towards a debt-free future. Remember that becoming debt-free is a process that requires discipline, perseverance, and conscious financial decision-making. By taking intentional steps and staying committed, you can achieve a debt-free lifestyle and unlock the many benefits it brings to your financial and personal life.

Conclusion: Sustaining Your Financial Freedom Journey

Congratulations! You've taken significant steps towards achieving financial freedom and securing a better future for yourself and your loved ones. Throughout this journey, you've learned the importance of financial literacy, setting clear goals, budgeting wisely, managing debt, and making informed investment decisions. Embracing a debt-free lifestyle and increasing your income have empowered you to take control of your finances and make conscious choices that align with your long-term aspirations. As you move forward on your financial freedom journey, it's essential to sustain your progress and continue building a secure and prosperous future.

Stay Committed to Your Goals: Remember the dreams and aspirations that led you on this financial freedom journey. Stay committed to your goals and use them as your guiding light during times of challenge or temptation. Every step you take towards your goals brings you closer to the life you envision.

Maintain a Healthy Budget: Continue to maintain a realistic budget that aligns with your financial objectives. Regularly review your spending habits and adjust your budget as needed to ensure you live within your means and save for your financial goals.

Invest Wisely: Continue to invest wisely and diversify your portfolio to manage risk. Keep yourself informed about the financial markets and stay attuned to the performance of your investments. Periodically reassess your investment strategy to ensure it aligns with your risk tolerance and long-term objectives.

Be Mindful of Debt: Even as you work towards a debt-free lifestyle, remain mindful of your credit usage. If you take on new debt, do so cautiously and with a clear plan for repayment. Prioritize paying off high-interest debts first and avoid falling back into the cycle of debt.

Reevaluate Your Financial Plan: Life is unpredictable, and circumstances change. Regularly review and reevaluate your financial plan to ensure it adapts to any life changes or economic fluctuations. Be open to adjusting your strategies as needed to remain on track towards your goals.

Build and Maintain an Emergency Fund: Continue building and maintaining an emergency fund to protect yourself and your family from unexpected financial setbacks. An emergency fund provides peace of mind and acts as a safety net during challenging times.

Seek Continued Financial Education: The journey to financial freedom is an ongoing process of learning and growth. Continue seeking financial education to deepen your knowledge and stay informed about evolving financial trends and strategies.

Celebrate Milestones and Progress: Celebrate your financial milestones and the progress you've made. Acknowledge your achievements and use them as motivation to keep moving forward. Rewarding yourself along the way reinforces positive financial behaviors.

Involve Your Family: Keep your family members involved in your financial journey. Share your goals and financial plans with them to foster a sense of shared purpose and collaboration. Encourage open discussions about money and financial decisions.

Give Back: As you achieve financial freedom, consider giving back to your community or supporting causes that are meaningful to you. Engaging in philanthropy can bring a sense of fulfillment and contribute to the well-being of others.

In conclusion, sustaining your financial freedom journey requires ongoing dedication, discipline, and mindful decision-making. Stay committed to your goals, maintain a healthy budget, and invest wisely. Be mindful of debt and continue to reevaluate your financial plan as circumstances change. Build and maintain an emergency fund and seek continued financial education. Celebrate your milestones and involve your family in your financial journey. As you progress, remember that achieving and sustaining financial freedom is not just about accumulating wealth; it's about living a life that aligns with your values and aspirations. It's about enjoying peace of mind, pursuing your passions, and creating a legacy that goes beyond money. Embrace your financial freedom journey with confidence and optimism, knowing that every step you take brings you closer to a brighter and more fulfilling future.

www.ingramcontent.com/pod-product-compliance
Lightning Source LLC
LaVergne TN
LVHW022311200926
848481LV00004B/1289
9798223636908